Copyright © 1970 by B.T.Batsford Ltd.
All rights reserved

Published in 1970 by The Viking Press, Inc.
625 Madison Avenue, New York, N.Y. 10022

SBN 670-40093-9

Library of Congress catalog card number: 77-125311

Filmset in Great Britain by Filmtype Services Limited, Scarborough Yorkshire
Made and printed in Great Britain by Jarrold & Sons Ltd., Norwich, Norfolk

Contents

Introduction   5

Near Buncrana, Co. Donegal   17
Errigal and the Dunlewey River, Co. Donegal   19
Sheephaven Bay and Muckish Mountain, Co. Donegal   21
Rossnowlagh, Co. Donegal   23
The Giant's Causeway, Co. Antrim   25
Dunluce Castle, Co. Antrim   27
Carnlough, Co. Antrim   29
Glenariff Glen, Co. Antrim   31
Carrickfergus Castle, Co. Antrim   33
City Hall, Belfast   35
Ardglass, Co. Down   37
Mountains of Mourne, Co. Down   39
Tyrella, Co. Down   41
Narrow Water Castle, Co. Down   43
Moyry Castle and Slieve Gullion, Co. Armagh   45
Clogher Head, Co. Louth   47
Monasterboice, Co. Louth   49
Meath Hunt, Cubbing Meet   51
Looking down at Dublin   53
The Four Courts, Dublin   55
Trinity College, Dublin   57
The Custom House, Dublin   59
Greystones, Co. Wicklow   61

Glendalough, Co. Wicklow 63

Ardmore Round Tower, Co. Waterford 65

The Rock of Cashel 67

St. Canice's Cathedral, Kilkenny 69

Innistioge, Co. Kilkenny 71

General View of Carlow 73

Wexford 75

St. Fin Barre's Cathedral and River Lee, Cork 77

Near Glengarriff, Co. Cork 79

Blarney Castle, Co. Cork 81

Evening at Killarney 83

Rossbeigh, Co. Kerry 85

Brandon Bay, Co. Kerry 87

MacGillycuddy's Reeks, Co. Kerry 89

Glenbeigh, Co. Kerry 91

Brandon Peak, Co. Kerry 93

Thomond Bridge and King John's Castle, Limerick 95

Lough Inagh, Co. Galway 97

Peat Bog near Maam Cross, Co. Galway 99

The Burren, Co. Clare 101

Derryclare Lough, Connemara 103

Ballynahinch River, Co. Galway 105

Near Costelloe, Connemara 107

Minaun Cliffs, Achill, Co. Mayo 109

Knocknarea, Co. Sligo 111

Acknowledgment 112

Introduction

Looking at a map of the world, Ireland is a small country; if physical extent, or population, were the criterion, we could never justify all that has been written about us, or our apparently exalted opinion of our own importance. But we believe our influence stretches far beyond the four provinces, for we have always been travellers like our ancestors, whether they came from Greece, Iberia or Northern Europe (via Britain). They have all had to fight for the right to call themselves Irishmen, a title not given easily, but once granted not lightly withdrawn. It is not surprising that we have sent our sons across the seas in every century, either because of adverse circumstances at home or because a particular call to service in foreign parts found a ready response. This was true of the teachers and preachers who beat a track across Europe in the dark ages and of the Crusaders who took to the Jerusalem road—generations later. The Wild Geese who joined the armies of Europe fled reluctantly at the end of the seventeenth century. Perhaps some of them knew the epigram composed by a Dominican friar who spent "seven dead winters abroad" at the beginning of the same century:

In France am I when I'm awake,
Asleep, I am in Ireland,
Little care I for wakefulness
Inducing sleep is my desiring.

The Irish surnames of the descendants of the Wild Geese crop up in the most unlikely parts of the Continent.

The greatest era of travelling began in the last century when—literally—millions sailed west to a new world—the Hy-Brasil of ancient legend—where hunger would be no more; a land of flowers and blazing sunshine. Those who survived the journey (and many never reached the promised land) may not have found it exactly as they had dreamed, but they did find work and opportunity and incomes from which they could spare a tithe for those who remained behind. The "money from America" has for generations been the jam on many an Irish family's bread, but it was also the tie that gave the third and fourth generation born, perhaps, in Boston, the right to call themselves Irish. At this time also, great numbers made their homes in Britain. Emigration was not always for a lifetime and you should not be surprised if the old man from whom you enquire the way in County Galway is as familiar with Commonwealth Avenue, 42nd Street, Piccadilly or the Bull Ring as he is with the place for which you are heading.

John Wesley called the world his parish, and the Irish claim to its children is hardly less wide. There are missionaries and soldiers, doctors and nurses, teachers and engineers in every part of the globe who look to this small island, not just with sentimentality, but with pride.

PREHISTORIC IRELAND

One of the first characteristics which a visitor will notice is the backward look. The Irishman's conversation is full of the past and this harking back to a golden age appears in the earliest literature of the country. The Irish are like Orpheus, forever looking back at the Eurydice they are attempting to bring home from the shades. To understand them and their countryside it is necessary to take a look at the history which has shaped them both.

We know little about the first Mesolithic—Middle Stone Age—men who settled in Ireland perhaps about 6000 B.C. but traces of their culture have been found, generally in the north east. They were followed about 3000 B.C. by the Late Stone Age or Neolithic settlers who were farmers and whose pottery remains have associated them with the same family of the Continent and Britain. They brought with them cereals which they planted in fenced fields and we know also that they brought cattle because no remains of wild cattle have been found from an earlier date.

Their prosperity is apparent from the monuments they have left in the two hundred or more court cairns or horned cairns, most of which are found in the north west—so called because they are gallery graves which incorporate a ritual unroofed court. Examples may be seen at Creevykeel and Deerpark, County Sligo, and at Browndod, County Antrim. Several centuries after the arrival of these first farmers, a new type of grave made its appearance; the collective chamber tombs or passage graves. One of the finest examples of this type of grave in

6

Western Europe is at Newgrange in the Boyne Valley. It was probably constructed about 2000 B.C. and consists of a passage and chamber, 79 feet long, with walls and roof of large slabs without mortar. A large circular cairn of stones covers the tomb and a retaining ring of massive slabs surrounds the base. There is an outer circle of standing stones—12 to 15 yards from the base. This outer circle averages 340 feet in diameter and encloses an area of about two acres. The cairn is about 36 feet high but appears more as it is set on the highest point of a ridge.

There are over 150 passage-graves surviving in Ireland and archaeologists believe that the builders came from Brittany and Iberia. The Beaker folk—so called because of their distinctive pottery—who colonized Britain so extensively, also landed in Ireland and heralded the Bronze Age. With this Age, commencing before 1500 B.C. which was about the date of the construction of the Egyptian Pyramids, came the first development from agriculture to manufacturing. As Ireland had exceptionally high deposits of gold and copper and Wicklow had attracted prospectors and miners as well as craftsmen from Europe, a substantial export trade was developed with Britain and the Continent in return for imports of daggers from Portugal, amber from the Baltic and glass and faience beads from the Eastern Mediterranean. Superb examples of gold ornaments of the period may be seen in the National Museum in Dublin. We know little of the houses of the period up to the middle Bronze Age since the upper walls were made of wood or wattle, but remains have been found at Lough Gur in County Limerick and at Lough Gara, near Boyle in County Roscommon, showing the outlines of "villages" of the period.

The late Bronze Age commenced after 950 B.C. to be followed by the early Iron Age when the art of iron-working arrived about 300 B.C. from the Upper Danube valley. Iron was used for tools and weapons and bronze continued to be the material of prestige objects. The mythology of the period suggests the extensive use of horses and chariots. This is one of the obscurest eras in the pre-history of Ireland, largely because the development of pottery did not keep pace in range or in quantity with metal objects. The burial places of these phases were less magnificent than the earlier eras and instead we have been bequeathed monuments in the 30,000 or 40,000 forts, of earth or stone, found in every part of the country. Many place-names in Ireland incorporate the Irish words used to describe different types of fort; *lios, rath, cathair, caiseal, dun*. The houses of the period were constructed within the forts and some continued to be occupied until the first century of our era—or later.

The outstanding feature of the early Iron Age is the development of a highly sophisticated abstract art in metal and stone which announced the arrival of the specifically Celtic phase of the European Iron Age. The cult-stones have wonderful spiral patterns and good examples may be seen at Turoe, near Loughrea, County Galway and at Castlestrange, near Athleague, County Roscommon.

MONASTIC IRELAND

By the end of the Iron Age, the Gaelic-speaking nation had evolved with its distinctive social and political institutions and its epic literature —a structure which was to survive until the seventeenth century. The Romans never came to Ireland, but caches of Roman silver have been found belonging to the first few centuries A.D.—the result of Irish piracy on the west coast of Britain. The pirates carried home more than precious metals; perhaps a Roman engineer to supervise a road-building programme and slaves whose iron shackles have been found as far west as County Roscommon. One of the slaves who arrived in 432 was called Patrick, and Ireland was never to be the same again after his arrival. The fall of the old religions is described by a poet who witnessed the change that was coming over the country:

> *Old haunts of the heathen*
> *Filled from ancient days*
> *Are but deserts now*
> *Where no pilgrim prays.*

The hermit life had a strong appeal in early Christian Ireland and there are many beehive huts of these centuries still standing, especially on the Dingle Peninsula. Magnificent examples are to be seen at the summit of Skellig Michael—a great sea rock off the Kerry coast. For the adventurous who will brave the sea journey from Portmagee— which can only be made in fair weather—and who are sure-footed enough to climb the rock steps, a pilgrimage to this, "the most western of Christ's fortresses in the ancient world," will be a rewarding and memorable experience. Here, among these tiny stone cells and oratories clinging to the rocks, one can see and sense the isolation and privations of the early monastic communities.

The great monasteries which became the "Holy Places" of Ireland, like Glendalough, Clonmacnoise, Kells and Monasterboice whose ruins show their sometime splendour, were folk colleges with considerable numbers of Anglo-Saxon and Frankish students. The pattern of life can be seen from the architectural remains. They are usually sited in some wild and beautiful place and inside the surrounding wall were half a dozen little oratories that were once linked up by streets of wooden houses. With the Viking invasions, a Round Tower is added with a doorway 12 or 15 feet up to which one could only ascend by ladder. The monasteries with their precious vessels, relics and manuscripts, were obvious targets for the heathen raiders and the Round Towers served as a refuge and a look-out. They have survived extraordinarily well and most monastic sites can show their tower intact or nearly so. At a later stage, a large church was added to the buildings and called a "cathedral".

The literature of the early Christian period is that of a people full of confidence, but the Viking invasions shattered that confidence, and the chaos they caused soon got into the prose. The first raid was in 795 A.D. and for the next two hundred years the Danes wrought incalculable depredation on the existing centres of culture. On the credit side they laid the foundations of most of the important Irish cities of to-day. In 841 A.D. their camp on the Liffey was turned into a permanent settlement which was to grow into the seaport of Dublin. There had been a town here from earlier times which Ptolemy in 140 A.D. had called Eblana, but its expansion began with the Danish occupation.

The final defeat of the invaders at the hands of King Brian Boru came at the Battle of Clontarf in 1014. Many of the Norse settlements, by this time Christian, remained to become part of the web of Irish life.

The coming of the Normans at the end of the twelfth century began seven hundred years of unhappy associations with our nearest neighbour England, from whence the Normans had come, and from this time began a period of conquest and plantation which was to last until 1690. In their conquest, the Normans erected massive castles at strategic points throughout the land and many well-preserved ruins remain like those at Trim, County Meath, and Adare, County Limerick. A few Norman castles are still inhabited.

The settlements of the seventeenth century finally sealed the fate of the old Gaelic culture and in the eighteenth-century Ireland's thinking, writing and building bore an unmistakable European pattern but with that distinctive stamp which was to make her Georgian buildings in particular one of the greatest national heritages.

GEORGIAN DUBLIN

The last half of the eighteenth century was Ireland's era of elegance, when architecture and public taste reached a greatness never achieved since, and it was then that the graceful houses and terraces of Armagh, Limerick, Cork, Waterford, Kilkenny and Dublin were built. Dublin is one of the finest of eighteenth-century cities, but it must disappoint many visitors at first glance. If one arrives by aeroplane the approach is unprepossessing—to say the least. It is a little better if the journey has been made by sea. The most unlikely approach is best; come down on this sleeping city on a summer morning across the Dublin mountains at Rathfarnham when the sun is chasing the mist away, and it will be love at first sight. Or steal in from the west through the Phoenix Park and a few minutes after you have passed the sprightly deer and grazing cattle which populate it, you will pass the most delightful railway station you are ever likely to see—at Kingsbridge—and along the banks of the Liffey to the city centre.

Apart from the two cathedrals, almost all the public buildings in Dublin are eighteenth- or early nineteenth-century and built of stone, as opposed to the domestic buildings of the era which are of brick. The distinguishing feature of all Dublin Georgian architecture is an exuberance—unknown elsewhere in Northern Europe—the rich and coloured traces of a Southern baroque past that England never knew. Superficially the streets and squares look like other cities built in the Augustan age, as the exotic touches are in the details; the doorcases and fanlights—each an individual. Some are expansive and highly decorated whilst others are modest and meticulous. Inside there are similar contrasts in the woodwork and the plasterwork. Dublin's plasterwork is her crowning beauty and was an art well learned by native craftsmen like Robert West, Edward Smyth, Michael Stapleton and Charles Thorp working in the second half of the eighteenth century and following the great Italian masters like the Francini brothers. Terrace houses of the period which from the outside are plain and resemble their neighbours, may contain ceilings and friezes of breath-taking beauty. A good example is 20 Lower Dominick Street which is an orphanage and may be visited. From the exterior it looks like its fellows in the street (those which remain) but the ceilings and walls are decorated with a superb fantasy of plaster birds, flowers and musical instruments—executed by Robert West. In the streets nearby on the north side of the Liffey are fine houses, many of which have outstanding plasterwork, although most of them have seen better days. Henrietta Street, one of the most beautiful streets in Dublin, has been allowed to deteriorate almost beyond recall, but excellent reclamations and restorations have been carried out in North Great Georges Street and Mountjoy Square, where a short-sighted lack of public policy has allowed the demolition of some magnificent houses in recent years. On the south side of the river the fine squares of Fitzwilliam and Merrion and the streets running off them and alongside have fared better as the houses have in very many cases been turned into prestige offices. But in this part of the city also there has been a running battle between conservationists who wish to save what is best in the city's architectural heritage against the inroads of developers.

There is such a wealth of good Georgian public buildings in Dublin that those mentioned here are ones which are distinguished internally as well as externally, and to which the public are freely admitted. The least accessible is the Marino Casino, which is the only non-functional building of the era in Dublin and is perhaps the most perfect building in Ireland. The parent house for which it was a pavilion has long since disappeared and it now stands lonely and forsaken—a dowager out-shining all debutantes. Thomas Ivory's Bluecoat School (now owned by the Incorporated Law Society) has a good Evie Hone east window in the Chapel, and in the Board Room a reproduction of the original ceiling by Charles Thorp. The Rotunda Hospital Chapel is without parallel in Ireland and is an example of this strong baroque influence which makes Irish plasterwork distinctive. Nearby is Charlemont House (1767), which is now the Municipal Art Gallery with a good collection of nineteenth- and twentieth-century paintings. The State

Apartments of Dublin Castle, which was the centre of British rule in Ireland for centuries, are very finely decorated. In the Bank of Ireland, which was the old Parliament Building, may be seen the House of Lords—much as it was in the eighteenth century. The public buildings of Trinity College were planned and built when space utilisation was not a prime consideration, and a walk through the college grounds will give one more of the feel of the Augustan age than anywhere else in Dublin. Newman House incorporates numbers 85 and 86 St Stephen's Green and has in the first, plasterwork by the Francini brothers and in the second work by one of the greatest of Irish stuccodores, Robert West. The National Gallery in Merrion Square, although nineteenth century, was built in classical style and the new extension is an example of how traditional proportions may be maintained with a modern interior. The churches of Dublin need a whole book to describe them. The two cathedrals, St Patrick's and Christ Church are twelfth century and both were extensively restored in the last century. St Mary's Pro-Cathedral is an imposing Greek Revival church completed in 1825. The dawn of the nineteenth century saw the unhappy union of the Irish parliament with Westminster, and resistance was to be built up during the century until the beginning of this one, when in 1916 what Yeats described as the "terrible beauty" was born and the country was divided into two political units. One bright light shining through a century which was to see famine on a scale unknown in the western world, was the passing of Catholic Emancipation in 1829 which was followed by the building of some notable churches and cathedrals throughout the country. Many of the earlier ones were in the classical style and later in the century the Gothic taste was to become almost universal, and produced splendid buildings like Maynooth College Chapel; St Mary's Cathedral, Killarney, and St Patrick's Cathedral, Armagh. The present century has seen some fine modern churches erected, particularly around Belfast and Cork in the provinces; Dublin has lagged behind in this respect.

GREAT HOUSES

It is one of the Irish virtues that we seldom set out self-consciously to entertain our visitors. We present ourselves and our beautiful countryside as they are and hope that our guests will like what they find;

but even in this paradise grey skies are not unknown and on such days when beaches, lanes and green fields lose their glamour, we can introduce you to some of our stately homes which are open to the public. In the north, many great houses are under the care of the Northern Ireland National Trust and there are two particularly fine houses in County Fermanagh; Castlecoole, which was designed by James Wyatt and is believed to be the finest example of his work, and Florence Court which is somewhat earlier. Castleward in County Down, beautifully situated on Strangford Lough is unique in having one half in classical style and the other in Strawberry Hill Gothic. There are not many seventeenth-century houses surviving in Ireland and Springhill at Moneymore in County Londonderry is such a house of great character.

Connaught was historically the underprivileged province, but it has several great houses to show. It has the most visited of Irish stately houses at Westport House, overlooking Clew Bay. Lough Cutra at Gort, County Galway, was designed by John Nash and has been lovingly and carefully restored from an almost ruinous condition. It is idyllically situated in woodland on the edge of a beautiful lake. In Munster there is the fine manor at Adare—one of the most attractive villages in Ireland. The formal gardens on the banks of the river Maigue are well laid out and the house contains work by the architect Pugin, who is better known as the designer of many fine Irish and English nineteenth-century churches. Riverstown House at Glanmire in the outskirts of Cork city presents one of those delightful surprises of travelling in Ireland. From the outside it is a modest-looking, reasonably-sized farmhouse. But inside it can show stucco of breathtaking beauty, the work of the Francini brothers. Copies of some of the finest plaques in the house were made to decorate Arus an Uachtarain, the President's residence in Phoenix Park, Dublin. Also in County Cork is Bantry House overlooking one of the country's loveliest bays.

The historic province of Leinster was partly covered by the Pale, the area of greatest English influence (those who lived outside it were "beyond the pale") and as a result there are very many great houses and Castles from the twelfth century onwards. Undoubtedly the finest open to the public is Castletown House at Celbridge, County Kildare, the first Palladian house in Ireland, built for William Connolly, Speaker of the Irish House of Commons. It is now the headquarters of the Irish

Georgian Society. Also in the same county is Carton, at Maynooth, which was the seat of the FitzGeralds, Dukes of Leinster, whose history is wrapped up in the story of the country from the Norman conquest onwards. This was the home of Lord Edward Fitzgerald, the ill-fated leader of the Rebellion of 1798. Tullynally Castle, near Castlepollard, County Westmeath, is the home of the Earls of Longford and is the largest castle in Ireland still lived in as a family home.

CLIMATE AND GARDENS

Ireland is blessed with a situation and climate which infuses colour into every landscape. The Atlantic, warmed by the Gulf Stream, ensures milder winters and moister summers than any other country of the same latitude. Irishmen have a particular sort of love/hate relationship with the rain. Generations of farming ancestors have taught them that there cannot be lush pastures and meadows without it, and a wet morning will invariably evoke some such greeting as "It's a grand, soft day". There is enough sunshine to ripen and bring bloom but not sufficient to bleach the soft colours the moist has bestowed. As a result of this temperate climate, although the Irish in general are not great gardeners, those who are have ideal conditions, and trees, shrubs and herbaceous plants from the hilly regions of much more southerly lands find the mildness and the amount of rainfall which they need. The soil has also had an influence on the type of plants grown as, by comparison with other European countries, there is little limestone and a lot of peat, and such conditions have made the rhododendron family at home everywhere. There are many other plants introduced to Irish gardens from South America and Australasia which flourish in peat.

Of the great gardens, the most excitingly placed is Ilnacullin on Garnish Island in the Bay of Glengarriff in County Cork. It is a dreamlike combination of woodland and formal settings with temples and pools, and has a climate which encourages plants that are rare in northern countries. The National Botanic Gardens in Dublin—which cover 27 acres—are well worth visiting and have played an important part in encouraging Irish gardening. Tollymore Forest Park at Newcastle, County Down, is a pleasure garden on the grand scale with many rare plants, shrubs and trees. The Japanese Gardens at Tully in County

Kildare are designed and laid out to show the life of man illustrated with quaint oriental symbolism.

There are many gardens surrounding great houses or planted by one family which are open to the public and these are some of them: Birr Castle, County Offaly; Mount Congreve, County Waterford (seen by appointment); Rowallane, County Down; Mount Usher and Powerscourt, County Wicklow. Mount Stewart near Newtownards, County Down, as well as its gardens of great magnificence and variety, has a superbly restored and decorated pavilion called the Temple of the Winds.

★ ★ ★

So this is Ireland, old and new, full of history but with an economy growing at a spanking pace, with gentle rolling hills and perhaps, hidden behind the next one, a fine modern factory working a 24-hour shift. We have never regarded work as a polite subject for conversation, and frequently there is more happening behind the scenes than appears to the casual observer. The joke goes that when an Irishman works late at the office, he tells his wife that he has been out with his secretary. . . . But, in spite of the strides forward, this is still a country where you can stop to bid a neighbour the time of day without causing a traffic jam. In moving from an almost exclusively agricultural economy we have avoided the worst aspects of the Industrial Revolution and we hope that we can keep our priorities right as we advance. Then perhaps around the corner will be the great age forecast by Saint Columbkille in the sixth century:

> *This new Eire shall be Eire the prosperous,*
> *Great shall be her renown and her power;*
> *There shall not be on the surface of the wide earth,*
> *A country found to equal this fine country.*

NEAR BUNCRANA, CO. DONEGAL

The mountainous Inishowen peninsula between Lough Swilly and Lough Foyle tapers towards Malin Head, the most northerly point in Ireland and is dominated by Slieve Snacht. The territory was once owned by the O'Dohertys, and at Buncrana there still stands the seat of the last proud lord of the clan, Sir Cahir O'Doherty. The keep of this ancient castle, built in 1430, is in good preservation.

There is good sea fishing in Lough Swilly, and there are brown trout in the River Crana. Between Buncrana and Fahan to the South, there is a three-mile stretch of golden sand.

Seven miles south of Fahan is the most interesting early structure in Ulster—the Grianan of Aileach. The grianans were fortresses into which the women were taken for safe keeping while the men were at the wars. This one is said to have been founded by Daghda about 1700 B.C. What one sees now is in part a nineteenth-century restoration. Its wall, tapering slightly to the top, is about 18 feet high and 13 feet thick, and there is one narrow entrance on the east side. Inside there is a stone gallery on which the sentinels kept watch. Around it are circular embankments which circumscribe the summit of Greenan mountain. It was at one time the royal residence of the O'Neills, Kings of Ulster and was destroyed at the beginning of the twelfth century by Murtagh O'Brien, King of Munster, in return for an O'Neill sacking of Kincora in Clare.

ERRIGAL AND THE DUNLEWEY RIVER, CO. DONEGAL

Errigal is a great quartzite cone with scarred and furrowed sides which only lacks a plume of smoke to make it a volcanic mountain. It is the highest in the county, 2,466 feet, and one of the most sporting climbs in Ireland. From Dunlewey Lake a direct ascent can be made to the top where there are two summits joined by a narrow ridge called "One Man's Path". The ascent takes about two hours, starting over heather and rough grass and then over loose screes. Under favourable conditions, most of the mountains of Ulster may be seen from the top and as far as Benbulben in Sligo. Sparkling below lie Lough Nacung and Dunlewey Lake, and to the north, Lough Altan with Aghlamore rising sheer from its waters.

Dunlewey and the Poisoned Glen are tweed-making centres. The Glen takes its name from the poisonous spurge (*genus Euphorbia*) which grows here and perhaps because of this the water in the glen is supposed to be unsuitable for drinking. At the head of the glen in the interior of the Derryveagh Mountains sheer cliffs form a huge amphitheatre. The great Glenveagh Deer Forest on either side of the valley is stocked with hundreds of deer.

SHEEPHAVEN BAY AND MUCKISH MOUNTAIN, CO. DONEGAL

Donegal has undoubtedly the most beautiful strands in Ireland. There are fine mountains like Muckish, always in brilliant shades of blue shown up by clusters of tidy white cottages and by the beaches, yellow as ripe corn.

Sheephaven and its neighbour, Mulroy Bay, are surrounded by a ring of delightful resorts; Dunfanaghy, Carrigart and Port-na-Blagh. A splendid view is from Creeslough through the neck of Sheephaven. The Atlantic drive round the Rosguill Peninsula is memorable, and it passes through the quiet resort of Downings and past lovely Tranarossan Bay. It is the valleys and inlets, sheltered and thickly wooded, which soften the landscape of the county, in many places rugged and hard as the Scottish Highlands.

Near Creeslough on the road to Carrigart, is a left turn to the bawn and keep of Doe Castle standing proud and lonely in a landlocked arm of the ocean, defended on the shoreward side by a rock-cut ditch formerly spanned by a drawbridge with a portcullised gatehouse. It was originally a stronghold of the MacSweeneys, and Eoghan Og MacSweeney was foster father to Red Hugh O'Donnell who lived here as a boy. There is an underground passage to the sea, and there are fine views from the ramparts.

ROSSNOWLAGH, CO. DONEGAL

This is a good centre for touring south Donegal, where every mile may offer a peninsula worth exploring, a hill worth climbing or the sight of the blue Atlantic scrubbing the tawny sand to a miraculous cleanness.

Men and motor cars shrink to insignificance on strands like these and the rolling waves grow larger to match the surrounding scale. But as well as such smiling beaches the county can show a snarling face as at Slieve League further along the coast. William Allingham, who was born in Ballyshannon, described the scene "that ocean mountain steep, six hundred yards in air aloft, six hundred in the deep". The best point from which to see this bulwark against the mighty waves is at the village of Bunglass, where one gets a ringside view of the two-thousand feet rock face. Although not the highest cliffs in Ireland, there is nothing of the kind to equal this spectacle.

THE GIANT'S CAUSEWAY, CO. ANTRIM

The Giant's Causeway is one of the world's strangest geological phenomena. The giant in question was Fionn Mac Coul who was building a causeway to Scotland. It was he also who was credited with forming Lough Neagh by taking up a handful of earth and throwing it in the Irish Sea, there to remain as the Isle of Man. Latter-day sceptics say that the causeway was formed by the cooling of lava which burst through the earth's surface, covering an area stretching to the island of Skye. The basalt cooled into thousands of prismatic columns, mostly six-sided, and others with various irregular numbers of sides. The cliffs are made of two beds of this basalt in columns, separated by a red band of iron ore formed by the decaying of the surface of the lava between periods of eruption.

There are three main sections: the Little Causeway, the Middle or Honeycomb Causeway and the Grand Causeway. Various formations have collected fanciful names: The Wishing Chair, The Amphitheatre, The Giant's Organ.

In the bay the *Gerona*, a ship of the Spanish Armada, was wrecked in 1588 and of 1300 souls aboard, only five survived. In recent years, divers have rescued coins, jewellery and precious relics from the seabed which have lain undisturbed since that terrible night. The disaster is commemorated in the name of the cove alongside the causeway—Port na Spaniagh.

DUNLUCE CASTLE, CO. ANTRIM

Dunluce Castle is said to have been built about 1300 by Richard de Burgh, Earl of Ulster, and was taken in 1560 by one of the larger-than-life characters of Irish history, Sorley Boy McDonnell. His name was as near as the English could get to *Somhairle Buidhe* (Yellow Charles). In the wars with Elizabeth I he was alternately courted by the Queen and warred upon.

The Castle rises from a rock, of which it almost seems a part; surrounded by the sea it is approached by a bridge across the intervening chasm. It is forbidding in its austerity set against a windswept background. Remains have been found here of early Christian and Viking occupation, and it was an obvious defensive site on this wild coast, being almost impregnable to men and arms. But the elements achieved what armies could not, and during the preparation of a Christmas banquet in 1639, a furious sea caused the collapse of the kitchen quarters and the servants fell to their doom on the rocks, or in the ocean. In one corner of the kitchen a beggar sat awaiting his portion of the feast, and this was the only part of the kitchens to remain standing. The embrasure where he was, is still pointed out as the Tinker's Window. Two years later, the McDonnells, Earls of Antrim, abandoned the Castle and it has been deserted ever since.

The precipitous white rocks beyond the Castle are pierced with numerous caves, some of which extend as much as two miles under the limestone cliffs.

CARNLOUGH, CO. ANTRIM

The 70 miles which separate Carrickfergus on Belfast Lough and the Giant's Causeway, is one of the most beautiful drives in the country. The Antrim Coast Road was designed by Sir Charles Lanyon in 1834 as a famine-relief scheme and its construction was a great feat of engineering. In places it runs within a few feet of the sea and where it cannot squeeze between the towering cliffs and the water, it goes through; through basalt at the Black Cave tunnel near Larne; through sandstone at Red Bay. The building of the road opened up the glens and the coast to visitors, and hamlets became seaside resorts. The glens still retain their distinct accents, traditions and character.

Carnlough, at the foot of Glencoy, is a delightful place with a fine crescent bay and a great stretch of golden sand. To the north of the bay is Garron Point, one of the most attractive headlands on this coast. On its wooded slopes stands Garron Tower, a castellated mansion built in 1848 for Lord Londonderry, which is now a school. Behind Carnlough there is a group of hills with several peaks over 1,000 feet.

GLENARIFF GLEN, CO. ANTRIM

The nine glens of Antrim are the boast of the county and this is the finest of them all. This lush valley is protected between high basaltic rock walls over which long waterfalls tumble. It stretches inland for about five miles, through the lower slopes, which are a multi-coloured pattern of fields, to the narrow upper valley, to which there is a small admission charge. For the energetic, there are a number of walks marked out with attractive wooden bridges and view-points. At Parkmore, the Ariffe river tumbles between thickly wooded banks over a series of picturesque falls—the Mare's Fall and the Fall of the Hooves.

The Glen opens into Red Bay where the village of Glenariff stands. Here the Antrim coast road passes through the "Red Arch" tunnel cut in the sandstone cliffs.

Scotland, which is never far away in County Antrim in sound or in space, can be seen across the North Sea.

CARRICKFERGUS CASTLE, CO. ANTRIM

This is one of the finest Norman Castles in these islands and for eight centuries has stood guard over the little port which was a gateway of Ulster.

The town takes its name from Fergus, King of Dalriada who set out from here to conquer the Picts and who is reputed to have brought with him Jacob's Pillow, as a talisman to bring good fortune to his venture, that stone which now rests under the Coronation Chair at Westminster. Since the Normans chose the rock of Fergus for their Castle, it has been an important centre of military and political power. The room in which King John stayed during much of his Irish campaign may still be seen. Edward Bruce and his brother, King Robert of Scotland, laid siege to the Castle and conquered it in 1315, but the English won it back after his defeat and death in 1317. The crusades were preached beneath its walls and the crusading banner flew from its towers. A stone on the harbourside marks the spot where King William III landed before the Battle of the Boyne in 1690, which was to have such significance for Ireland, and indeed for Europe. It is only in recent years that the Castle, for the first time in its history, ceased to house a military garrison.

There are two courts enclosed by a curtain wall which follows the natural outline of the peninsula. The massive keep against the west wall of the inner court has walls nine feet thick.

CITY HALL, BELFAST

Unlike most cities of its size, Belfast's river does not provide a focus where roads and streets come to a logical conclusion. The industrialized banks of the Lagan, which improbably runs from South to North, is well to the right of centre and instead, everything in this busy city begins and ends at the City Hall. It is a large impressive Renaissance-style building, a monument to the industrial prosperity of the city at the beginning of this century, at a time when few other parts of the country had been touched by industrialization. It is one of several noble nineteenth- and twentieth-century buildings in the city. The Cathedral of St. Anne, which was begun in 1899, is a dignified Romanesque Church. The Parliament Building at Stormont occupies a magnificent site approached by a broad processional avenue. The Queen's University is a fine Tudor-Gothic building.

ARDGLASS, CO. DOWN

To anyone born in Ulster the name of Ardglass is almost certainly associated with the homely herring which has made the town well-known, not only in its own country, but as far away as the Baltic and the ports of Russia. Ardglass has a great seafaring past and was one of the main ports in the east, carrying on a brisk wine trade with France. Traces of earthworks—the Green Height which the name means—are probably the remains of a Norman palisaded fort. The town early became an English settlement and remained one when English influence had declined in Ulster. Its history is boasted in the five fourteenth- to sixteenth-century "castles" which remain in various states of decay, adaptation or preservation. These buildings were in fact part fortress, part warehouse. Jordan's Castle, or Shane's Castle, as it has been known since 1916, the best preserved, is a square tower 70 feet high with four storeys, and is now a national monument. It is thought to have been built by a trading company in the reign of Henry IV. It was defended by Simon Jordan for three years against Hugh O'Neill, Earl of Tyrone, in the sixteenth century.

MOUNTAINS OF MOURNE, CO. DOWN

In sweeping down to the sea the mountains of Mourne leave little room for the attractive towns which lie snugly in between to spread themselves. The mountains are not masked by foothills like so many other Irish ranges. At Newcastle, built on a patch borrowed from mountains and sea, they are seen in all their splendour. There are no great peaks— Slieve Donard, the highest, is 2,900 feet, and only two have jagged and broken summits, Binyon and Bernagh. The others are round-topped and can be climbed without great difficulty, the finest climb being from Tollymore Park up the shoulder of Comeragh. At the summit the valleys fall away in both directions leaving one on a ridge hundreds of feet high.

Newcastle is Ulster's most attractive resort, splendidly situated at the western end of the sandy beach fringing Dundrum Bay. It has two 18 hole golf courses—one of them the famous Royal County Down Championship course. The "New Castle", built by Felix Magennis in 1588 to replace an older one, where the river Shimna enters the sea, has completely disappeared.

TYRELLA, CO. DOWN

This splendid beach is a favourite resort for bathers and picnickers in the fine Bay of Dundrum in County Down. The area south of Downpatrick is the barony of Lecale—an ancient Norman territory dotted with castle keeps with modern farmhouses grafted on. From here many crusading knights set off on their marathon trek across Europe to Jerusalem.

The "Kingdom of Mourne" is the friendliest of places. It lies off the main traffic routes and was for centuries relatively inaccessible and has, as a result, preserved older ways than many other parts of Ulster. There is a family air and intimacy about it which draws visitors warmly back to it year after year.

In the grounds of Downpatrick Cathedral is the reputed grave of the three principal saints of Ireland, Patrick, Brigid and Colmcille, marked by a large granite boulder inscribed with a cross and the name PATRIC. Saul, close by, is the place where St. Patrick landed in 432 to begin his mission in Ireland.

NARROW WATER CASTLE, CO. DOWN

Carlingford Lough and the Newry water have been the channel to Ulster for successive invaders; megalithic man, Dane, Norman and Saxon have all come this way. The control of this access was always important, and one of the many Irish castles built to King John's order was at Carlingford. Newry has traditionally been an important trading centre and the original castle on this rock connected to the shore by a causeway, was built by Hugh de Lacy in 1212. The Duke of Ormonde built the present structure in 1663. It commands a beautiful stretch of lough shore and rises grandly from the water beside the Newry-to-Warrenpoint road. From the wooded hills behind, one looks across the 300 yards that divide Ireland politically, to the Cooley peninsula which was once the fiefdom of Cuchulain, the Ulster hero in the days of the Red Branch Knights. The greatest of Celtic sagas was the Tain-Bo-Cuailgne which told of the raid made on Ulster by the rest of Ireland to capture the Brown Bull of Cooley.

MOYRY CASTLE AND SLIEVE GULLION, CO. ARMAGH

This is the stage on which one of the great scenes of legend was acted—the death of Cuchulain of the Red Branch Knights, defending his province against the southern kings. It had been foretold that he would lift the curse which had been laid on Ulster by Macha. But it was only when he was mortally wounded by a spear, and had bound himself to a stone pillar so that he might die upright facing the enemy, and a raven had alighted on his shoulder letting his followers know that he was dead, that the curse was lifted from the warriors of Armagh. They then proceeded to a victory without parallel in the annals of Ireland.

Slieve Gullion has two prehistoric graves; the one at the northern end is a cairn about 50 feet across and about 10 feet high. The other at the summit, known as Calliagh Birra's House, is twice as wide and has a passage grave with a corbelled circular chamber. It is worth climbing to the top if only for the splendid view over a great stretch of countryside which is rich in remains from the earliest times.

Below the mountain is the strategic Gap of the North which was the main entry to Ulster from the South—the Dublin to Belfast railway still runs through it. The sturdy little keep of Moyry (or Moyra) in the foreground, was built in 1601 by Lord Deputy Mountjoy to defend the Pass between the Pale and the Gaelic North. It is only 24 feet square, with rounded corners, musketry loop-holes and a cobbled floor.

CLOGHER HEAD, CO. LOUTH

Louth is the smallest, but among the most prosperous counties in Ireland, with its two fine towns of Dundalk and Drogheda. Dundalk was historically a frontier town, separating the Pale—the English-ruled area to the south, from the Irish north. Now the allegiances are reversed, but Dundalk remains a border town. Drogheda on the Boyne is close to the site of the most important battle in the history of these islands in the seventeenth century. The Battle of the Boyne in 1690 led to the final overthrow of the Stuarts and the establishment of a limited monarchy in England.

Between the two is the pretty fishing village of Clogher. The harbour and pier, called Port Oriel, are separated from the village by Clogher Head, and close by there is a glorious mile and a half long strand.

In the face of the head is "The Red Cave", so called from a reddish fungus which grows over it, but local legend maintains the colour comes from a brutal massacre committed there in the seventeenth century.

MONASTERBOICE, CO. LOUTH

The settlement of Monasterboice was founded, probably in the fifth century, by St. Buithe about whom little is known, but who gave his name to the monastery, *Mainistear Bhuithin* in Irish, and in a round-about way also to the river Boyne in whose valley the community flourished. Here there are two of the best of all Irish high crosses, which as well as honouring the central event of Christianity, were means of instruction to the unlettered, frequently in a light-hearted fashion. The carving below the centre shows the Archangel Michael weighing souls in the balance while the devil lies on his back and tips the scales. The apple which Eve is presenting in the bottom panel is as tempting as when it was carved a thousand years ago. This is the east face of Muireadach's Cross, over 17 feet high, which bears an inscription in Irish on the other side: "A prayer for Muireadach who caused the cross to be made'. There was an abbot of this name who died in 922. The West or Tall Cross is over 21 feet high and is also richly ornamented. The round tower can be climbed and must have been the tallest in the country when complete with its conical cap.

MEATH HUNT, CUBBING MEET

Hunting has a long and noble history in Ireland. The huntsman was an important dignitary of the chieftains' courts of the middle ages where his functions ranged wider than the field of sport. His bugle was the horn of an ox, valued at one pound, and his protection extended as far as the sound of his horn could reach. Whenever his oath was required he swore by his horn, hounds and leashes. It was his duty to accompany the army on the march and to sound the alarm and signal of battle. The Normans introduced the "Art of Venerie" and order and ceremonial to the hunting field.

From the sixteenth century there was a great appreciation of Irish horses as hunters. General Markham writing in 1616 refers to the Irish pony as having a fine head, strong neck, well-cast body, good limbs, sure of foot, nimble in dangerous places, and of lively courage.

The "royal county" of Meath is fine hunting country with large fields intersected by deep broad ditches for drainage, which provide exciting jumps for the most cool-headed rider and sure-footed horse.

LOOKING DOWN AT DUBLIN

One of the joys of Dublin, to use an Irishism, is that it is so easy to get out of. From the heart of the city one can see the haymaking on the side of the Dublin mountains, which is as it should be for the capital of a country whose principal industry is agriculture. In less than half-an-hour from O'Connell bridge heading north, west or south, one can find greenness and peace all around. Howth on the right of the photograph which looks like an island but is a steep headland, is a bonus that only the most benign gods would give to an already beautifully situated city. The gardens of Howth Castle are open to the public where the rhododendrons are justly celebrated, and the village and harbour are delightful. The views from the Summit are splendid and at night the chain of light around Dublin Bay turns the city into a fairyland.

Westward one comes to the Phoenix Park with its broad acres and wandering deer. To the south is the beautiful county of Wicklow, and whether one follows the coast or takes the inland roads, this is a countryside to be remembered.

THE FOUR COURTS, DUBLIN

James Gandon's two great buildings dominate the north side of the river Liffey, the Custom House and the Four Courts. Both suffered in the "Troubles" and have been restored, and both set that low skyline which was one of Dublin's most attractive features and has only been ruptured by towers of glass and concrete in the city centre in recent years. It is ironical that until the age of town planners this convention was faithfully observed. The Courts are about a mile west of O'Connell Bridge where the river makes a slight curve, and originally the wings projected six feet beyond the central block. Unfortunately the fine stucco decoration in the Great Hall perished in the catastrophe of 1922.

Near the Fourt Courts the Liffey is spanned by its finest curved bridges which have so far escaped being flattened and widened. The Guinness barges, like the Clonsilla, no longer chug along the water and Dublin's best-known product now speeds to the port by more efficient means.

TRINITY COLLEGE, DUBLIN

Twenty paces from the bustling traffic of College Green transports the visitor to the Front Square of the "College of the Holy and Undivided Trinity near Dublin". The city has come to meet and surround it since Queen Elizabeth I established the University of Dublin in 1591. No university could be better placed, and town and gown pursue a happy co-existence. The Front Square, comprising of Parliament and Library Squares, is surrounded by the principal public buildings of the college. The Public Theatre (1791) and the Chapel (1798) are decorated with fine examples of plasterwork, which in the Theatre is the work of Michael Stapleton, one of the greatest of Irish stuccodores. The Dining Hall, where students who live in "rooms" in the college dine each evening, was designed by Richard Cassels and completed in 1761. The Campanile houses the great bell of the college and the smaller "Provost's Bell" which may have come from the monastery of All Hallows, on the site which Trinity College now occupies. "The Rubrics" in the background are the oldest buildings in the university.

In the Library are the famous illuminated Celtic manuscripts including the Book of Kells, which is generally believed to be the world's most beautiful manuscript.

THE CUSTOM HOUSE, DUBLIN

The noblest of Dublin's eighteenth-century public buildings, the Custom House, was designed by James Gandon and completed in 1791. It was the outward and visible sign of the prosperity and the elegance of the era. Dublin was then the second largest city of the British Empire and the seventh in the world. Its merchants were prosperous under a progressive Irish parliament and they and the aristocracy were building splendid town houses to match their affluence. But it was not to last; nine years after the opening of the Custom House the Act of Union was passed, bringing to an end the city's brief glory, and a long slow decline set in.

The building was burnt to a shell in 1921, but it was faithfully restored.

GREYSTONES, CO. WICKLOW

This is an ideal centre for seeing the "Garden of Ireland", as County Wicklow is called. It is a pleasant town (a few miles south of Bray Head) with a fine shingle beach. It retains much of the atmosphere of a fishing village and is a commuter town with a good train service to Dublin, as well as being a favourite resort with those who favour the drier east coast. It has little in common with the more exuberant holiday towns of the south and west.

Within easy driving distance is the village of Enniskerry, one of the prettiest in the country, with its demesne of Powerscourt, which has Ireland's greatest formal garden. The grounds are open to the public, and the Waterfall, tumbling some 400 feet is a splendid sight. Near Ashford on the road to Wicklow town are the romantic gardens of Mount Usher laid out along a reach of the river Vartry, planted with trees and flowering shrubs from every corner of the world.

GLENDALOUGH, CO. WICKLOW

The Valley of the Two Lakes was chosen by Saint Kevin in the sixth century as a remote spot for his community of anchorites. No longer isolated and within easy driving distance of Dublin, it is a magnet for large numbers of visitors every day of the year. But even crowds of sightseers cannot dispel the brooding atmosphere of mystery which haunts this lovely glen. On a dull day this sacred precinct can evoke the most profound melancholy.

The monastic city once housed a great school and thousands of students flocked to it. The arched entrance in the protective surrounding wall is still in a good state of preservation after nearly a thousand years. The Round Tower is in perfect condition and the ninth-century St. Kevin's Kitchen, as one of the Chapels is commonly called, is complete with its stone roof, which is unusual as most Irish Churches of the time were thatched. Kevin's Bed is a cave above the Upper Lake which is reached by boat and is said to have housed the saint.

The Vikings pillaged the town at least four times and it ceased to be an important monastic centre when the See was absorbed into that of Dublin in 1214.

ARDMORE ROUND TOWER, CO. WATERFORD

No holiday camp developer could improve on the sites chosen for the early monastic settlements. Saint Declan, who founded Ardmore, had a wide choice because he arrived even before Saint Patrick. It must be almost as peaceful now as when he chose this lovely hill. On either side there are beautiful strands, and all around is green and fertile.

Declan's Oratory, or Tomb, a rude hut, has been a place of pilgrimage for centuries. The Cathedral, of nave and chancel, includes work from the tenth to the fourteenth centuries. Its most interesting feature is the Romanesque arcading on the outside of the west wall which can just be seen on the extreme left of the photograph. This is unique in Ireland and is of two rows one above the other with biblical scenes carved in the stone, similar to the ancient high crosses.

The Round Tower, which is one of the most perfect, is also unique in having four projecting beltings dividing it into as many storeys. It is 97 feet high and 15 feet in diameter at the base, and the round-headed door is, as usual, placed high above ground level. Inside is a series of projecting stones carved into grotesque heads.

THE ROCK OF CASHEL

As one rounds a bend on the main Dublin to Cork road the sweep of the broad fertile plains of Tipperary is broken by a mirage, a majestic rock crowned by a fairy-tale castle. This natural fortress standing guard over the Golden Vale was the capital and seat of the kings of Munster for 700 years, until 1101, when it was granted to the Church. From the time when St. Patrick baptised King Aengus here, the twin Swords of Church and State ruled and several of the kings were also bishops and the bishops warriors.

Within the enclosing wall there is a tenth-century round tower, an eleventh-century high cross, a castle and a gothic cathedral. But the gem of the Rock is Cormac's Chapel, seen in the centre of our photograph, tucked in an angle between the south transept and the choir. It was built by Cormac, king-bishop of Cashel, and consecrated in 1134. It is the most perfect example of the Irish Romanesque style, and with its stout stone roof has withstood the disasters which wrecked the Cathedral, built a century later.

ST. CANICE'S CATHEDRAL, KILKENNY

Kilkenny is the fairest among Ireland's small cities. It is steeped in history which it makes no attempt to conceal, and no Irish town can match its record of restoration and renovation. This is a town which is loved and cherished by its citizens.

Saint Canice founded his Church here in the sixth century and gave the town its name, Canice's Church. The present Cathedral, which dates from the thirteenth century, is believed to be on the same site. It is built on a gentle hill overlooking Irishtown, where little houses cluster together under its shadow. Like Kilkenny's other buildings, it has been restored and repaired over the centuries. There was a major restoration after Cromwell's visitation when the Cathedral was used as a stable, and also in the last century when Sir Thomas Deane was called in as architect. But in spite of a troubled history, the building is, on the whole, as it originally was, and it is unusually consistent in style and symmetrical in plan. The Early English west window and the quatrefoil clerestory windows, the east window and the fine groining of the central tower, are good examples of their period.

The round tower belongs to the period of Canice's original Church.

INNISTIOGE, CO. KILKENNY

The name means Tighe's Island and nearby is the well-wooded demesne of Woodstock, which was the home of the Tighe family. The house, once famous, was damaged by fire in 1922. In the parish church is Flaxman's tomb for Mary Tighe who, as author of "Psyche" had a short-lived fame as a poetess.

This is one of the most attractive towns in Leinster with the lime-shaded green and climbing streets. It is situated in one of the prettiest parts of the Nore Valley. The river is dotted with islands, and winds between wooded banks flanked by hills. In the town it is crossed by a ten-arched bridge ornamented on the Southern side by Ionic pillars.

The clock-faced tower of the parish church in the centre belonged to the Augustinian Monastery founded here in 1210.

GENERAL VIEW OF CARLOW

The Norman castle in Carlow is now a noble ruin but it might have survived in its entirety had it not been for an "improving" doctor who was its tenant in 1814. He wished to use the building as an asylum for the insane and used gunpowder to remove some inner walls. In the process the foundations were disturbed and most of the castle fell in. The west wall and flanking towers now stand guard over the bridge which, in days gone by, was a gateway to the Pale.

It was in its rôle as guardian of the Pale that Carlow's history was made. It was a stronghold of the Anglo-Normans and was walled in 1361. Thereafter it was frequently a scene of struggles, sieges and burnings.

St. Mary's Parish Church was believed to be the subject of Swift's couplet:

> *High Church and a low steeple,*
> *A poor town and proud people.*

It may be as a result of this, that the spire (seen in the centre) was added.

The Cathedral of the Assumption, a Gothic-Revival building, was the first cathedral to be built after Catholic Emancipation.

Two miles east of the town, at Browne's Hill, is a dolmen with the largest capstone in the country, estimated to weigh a hundred tons.

WEXFORD

To cross the fine modern bridge into Wexford town is to land in Irish history. Ptolemy, the geographer, in the second century A.D. called it Menapia, in Irish it is *Loch Garman*, and the modern name is an anglicized form of the name given by the Vikings to the settlement they established here and ruled for two centuries. It was the first town captured by the Anglo-Normans in 1169. Cromwell treated it just a little less badly than Drogheda, and in 1798 it was the heart of the rising.

Its narrow streets belie the busy seaport and manufacturing centre which it is to-day. To opera lovers throughout the world its name is known for the Festival held each October when two lesser-known operas are produced in its intimate and delightful eighteenth-century Theatre Royal, with international principals and a devoted and disciplined local chorus.

ST. FIN BARRE'S CATHEDRAL AND RIVER LEE, CORK

Ireland's third city grew from the monastic community founded in the sixth or seventh century where the beautiful River Lee empties into one of the greatest of natural harbours. Like other monasteries, it suffered from the raids of the Vikings in the ninth century, but in 917 these erstwhile enemies returned to found a settlement which was the real beginning of the city as a commercial centre. In the seventeenth century traders from all over Europe came to Cork for salt fish, salt butter and salt meat. In the eighteenth and nineteenth centuries, glass and silver ware were made here. They enjoyed a high repute and are now much sought after by collectors. Nowadays it is a busy industrial centre, yet few cities could retain such charm and intimacy side by side with rapid progress.

Saint Fin Barre's Cathedral was completed a hundred years ago in the year in which the Church of Ireland was disestablished. It was designed by W. Burges, a Victorian architect whose work has been neglected until recent years, and it is built in the French Gothic style.

NEAR GLENGARRIFF, CO. CORK

One of the joys of travelling in south-west Ireland is to drive along a bleak and lonely road and in the twinkling of an eye to be surrounded by lush greenery, life and colour. The experience is as in an O'Casey play when one plunges from high comedy to stark tragedy and the tears of joy serve also for the sorrow. The road to Glengarriff from Killarney through Kenmare hugs the side of the Caha mountains and in places is hewn through the rock in long tunnels. Ahead is the vast spread of Bantry Bay, then suddenly you are in Glengarriff, gay and warm and full of activity.

The climate is exceptionally mild and everywhere there are palms, azaleas, passion flowers and sub-tropical shrubs. The lovely arbutus also thrives here, and the hedges are of fuchsia and rhododendron.

The name means "the rugged glen" and our photograph shows a spot beside the village where the ruggedness has not been tamed and nature's garden still holds sway.

BLARNEY CASTLE, CO. CORK

Blarney Castle was originally a fortress of the MacCarthys of south Munster and it withstood several sieges from the fifteenth century to the seventeenth century.

It was one of the MacCarthys who is reputed to have given the word blarney to the English language. Cormac MacDermot MacCarthy was repeatedly asked by Carew, the deputy of Queen Elizabeth I, to renounce the system by which the Irish clans elected their chief and to take the tenure of his lands from the Crown. While seeming to agree, he put off the implementation from day to day "with fair words and soft speech", until Elizabeth declared, "This is all blarney, what he says he never means".

The Castle is an 85-feet keep built on a rock. Beneath it are two caves, one of which has been artificially enlarged, possibly to form a dungeon. The stone, which is reputed to confer eloquence on all who kiss it, is mounted just below the battlements, and to reach it one has to lean over backwards, grasping an iron railing, from the parapet walk.

The view from the top of the Castle over the wooded hills of Muskerry is very fine.

EVENING AT KILLARNEY

Killarney is Ireland's original tourist attraction—it has been visited and admired for centuries. Sir Richard Hoare, in his *Tour of Ireland* in 1806 wrote: "It is out of the power of the pen or pencil to do its beauties justice, I shall not venture on an attempt where my failure would be certain". In spite of this self-imposed restriction he proceeded, like many others since, to describe the indescribable. Killarney has so much to offer in one place, mountains and lakes, marvellously planted woods and waterfalls, a national park and excellent hotels. To see the beauty spots close by, requires travelling first by jaunting car, then by rowing boat through the lakes (motor boats are *verboten*) and on horseback up the Gap of Dunloe. A motor car will take you further afield along roads overhung with ancient trees and lined with *rhododendron ponticum* which flourishes in ideal conditions here—a peaty soil and humid atmosphere. Remains have been found showing that the rhododendron was at home in Killarney 250,000 years ago, in the warmer periods of the Ice Age. There is also the pleasure of walking through a great natural park with its population of 200 Red deer and over 1,000 Sika deer.

ROSSBEIGH, CO. KERRY

To those who seek solitude on holiday here is perfection, with miles of golden beach, backed by sandhills. Rossbeigh peninsula stretches for two miles into Dingle Bay and is matched by Inch which comes down to meet it from the Northern peninsula. At the north end of the sandhills is a tower built in the last century as a guide mark for ships entering the fine Castlemaine Harbour.

To the east is Caragh Lake, a beautiful lough four miles long through which the Caragh river flows, and there are splendid walks along the valley of the river to Blackstone Bridge, a distance of about a mile and a half. The hills on the east side are dotted with little lakes and can be reached from a small road following the north-eastern shore.

Killorglin on the Killarney road is the scene of the annual Puck Fair in August which lasts for three days—"Gathering Day", "Puck Fair Day", and "Scattering Day". The focus of the celebrations is King Puck, a crowned and be-ribboned goat, who presides over the business and celebrations from a dais in the centre of the town.

BRANDON BAY, CO. KERRY

From this bay St. Brendan set out on his epic voyage across the uncharted seas. Further west on the Dingle Peninsula is a still more important landmark in the history of Irish Christianity—the Oratory of Gallarus. This little upturned boat of a building is one of the country's most important shrines. A tiny chapel of unmortared stone slabs with walls three feet thick, it was probably built in the eighth century and is still weatherproof more than a thousand years later. It stands unpretentiously, surrounded by little fields, with dry stone walls, like any farm outhouse without a thatched roof, but it represents the virile faith of a remote people in the days before an all-embracing uniformity spread across Europe.

This area has literally hundreds of other early remains, including several beehive oratories, and at least twelve large stone crosses. There are also numerous standing stones and ringed forts.

MACGILLYCUDDY'S REEKS, CO. KERRY

The Gap of Dunloe separates the Purple mountain from the Reeks. It is a magnificent defile which is part of the visitors' tour of Killarney. It must be seen on foot or on the ponies provided. Great rocks rise on either side of the road which runs alongside a turbulent stream and at one point the guides send echoes flying around the hills with their bugles.

The awesome Macgillycuddy's Reeks can boast Ireland's highest mountain—Carrantuohill (3,414 feet). It is best ascended from Gortbue on the north side at the mouth of the Hag's Glen, then through the glen and up the Devil's Ladder to the summit. Superb views take in the Shannon and County Limerick and County Cork to the east. There are many cliffs for the rock climber.

The lonely Lough Acoose is on the west end of the range and the ridge walk, best commenced from here, across Skregmore, Beenkeragh, Caher and Carrantuohill, is very fine.

GLENBEIGH, CO. KERRY

The "Ring of Kerry" road skirts the broad Iveragh Peninsula and the circle from Kenmare to Killarney is over 90 miles and has the most outstanding scenery in the Kingdom of Kerry. There is a backbone of towering mountains and few roads cross the interior. The pastel colours of the peaks contrast splendidly with the oases of greenery in the lowlands.

Glenbeigh, the Glen of the Birch Trees, takes its name from the lovely valley of the same name. The surrounding hills, known as the "Glenbeigh Horseshoe", provide one of the finest mountain walks in the county, of about 20 miles. Commencing from Seefin, which has associations with Fionn, the hero of Celtic legend, it leads past lake-filled cirques and glacial corries to Drung Hill. The road on the steep north side of Drung Hill leads from Glenbeigh to Cahirciveen and gives a spectacular view of the Dingle Peninsula and the now deserted Blasket Islands. The last inhabitants were moved from these islands to the mainland in 1953, but life on the Blaskets is familiar to many far beyond Ireland from the outstanding story-telling tradition of the islanders which produced *Twenty Years A-Growing*, *The Islandman* and *Peig*.

BRANDON PEAK, CO. KERRY

This part of the Dingle Peninsula is rich in associations with one of the most colourful of Irish saints—Brendan the Navigator. Mount Brandon is named after him and on the summit are some contemporary remains of his retreat.

Brendan was born in this district about 486. His life and the story of his voyage is told in *Navigationis Brendani*, which was a mediaeval best seller, translated into all important European languages. In 551 he set out with his companions to find Hy-Brasil, the paradise of the west, where it was said the sun shone all the year round, and fruit and flowers were as plentiful as in the Garden of Eden. Brendan's hopeful travelling was as exciting as his arrival. He met a floating mountain "the colour of silver, harder than marble, of substance of the clearest silver"—later Atlantic sailors were to be less lyrical about icebergs, and he was said to have celebrated the holy mysteries on the back of a whale. On arrival he found Hy-Brasil was divided by a mighty river so wide that it could not be crossed—a possible description for the Mississippi. Certain Christian relics found on the eastern seaboard of the United States have been linked with the Irish tradition because of their Celtic appearance.

THOMOND BRIDGE AND KING JOHN'S CASTLE, LIMERICK

To many visitors who arrive by air, Limerick, as the closest city to Shannon, is the gateway to Ireland. It is a good place to meet that blending of the old and new which marks almost all Irish cities. The main thoroughfare, O'Connell Street, in its length of $\frac{3}{4}$ mile, has fine stores at one end, and, at the other, splendid Georgian houses now mainly used as offices. St. Mary's Cathedral, the tower of which can be seen on the left, was founded in 1194 by Donal Mor O'Brien who granted his own palace for the purpose. The unique feature of the Cathedral is the fifteenth-century misericords with their grotesque and amusing carvings. In the mid-west of Ireland you will find constant reminders of the power and influence of the O'Briens, one of the greatest of Irish families, descended from King Brian Boru who finally overcame the Danes at the Battle of Clontarf in 1014.

King John visited Limerick in 1210 and ordered the castle be built "to watch towards Thomond" (the O'Brien country), and a bridge to span the Shannon.

LOUGH INAGH, CO. GALWAY

Stretching along a glacial valley, Glen Inagh keeps the peace between the Maamturks and the Twelve Bens, and the road which follows the shore of Lough Inagh leads north and east to the lovely fjord-like Killary Harbour and the village of Leenane, which is a fisherman's paradise. To the north and west is Kylemore, one of the best-known beauty spots of Connemara.

This wild and beautiful countryside has an enchanting sense of timelessness. The farmers will say that the hay in their pocket handkerchief fields would not be ready for turning much before midday. The visitor will wonder why the dew is heavier than in other places, but in a few days he, too, will have his priorities right. There are excellent hotels and good roads, but most important of all are the charming friendly people who may speak Irish to each other, but have equal facility in the "strangers' tongue". It is essential to adopt the pace of Connemara when you are visiting it or else you will miss the little roads which lead nowhere, except perhaps to a view which you will remember for the rest of your days.

PEAT BOG NEAR MAAM CROSS, CO. GALWAY

The traditional social life of Ireland centred on the turf fire, with its rich pungent smoke which pervaded the air all around the clusters of cottages when neighbours went "rambling" (visiting) of an evening. In many parts of the country, hand-saved turf, as in the photograph, is still the main source of fuel, while the city dweller buys his compressed briquettes in take-away bundles. Mechanisation has opened up the major bogs of the midlands, providing fuel for electricity generation and peat moss for the gardener.

Each area of the country has its own variety of purple heather, which provides the background for the brilliant white bog cotton or *ceannabhan*, seen in the foreground.

Maam Cross is the crossroads of Connemara, surrounded by little lakes as attractive as their names. The road westwards to Recess passes through some splendid scenery following the shores of Lough Shindilla and Lough Oorid, the Maamturk hills are on the right and the Twelve Bens loom majestically ahead.

THE BURREN, CO. CLARE

Surely the loneliest but one of the most impressive corners of Ireland, the Burren covers about 50 square miles of north-west Clare. It is a fascinating area of bare limestone hills and plateaux whose karsts are well known to botanists, geologists and antiquarians. In the thin soil of its hollows there survives the most remarkable collection of diverse types of flora to be found in the country, and a visit in the Spring when the tiny flowers dare to compete with the harsh grey is a joy to remember.

John Betjeman caught the atmosphere of the Burren:

> *Stony seaboard, far and foreign,*
> *Stony hills poured over space,*
> *Stony outcrop of the Burren,*
> *Stones in every fertile place,*
> *Little fields with boulders dotted,*
> *Grey-stone shoulders saffron-spotted,*
> *Stone-walled cabins thatched with reeds,*
> *Where a Stone Age people breeds*
> *The last of Europe's stone age race.*

The bleakness of the country is emphasised by the solitary rocks, some mushroom shaped, which dot the landscape like the toys of an untidy giant.

Lisdoonvarna, at the Southern tip of the Burren, is a well-known spa, and the surrounding countryside has a complex system of limestone caves and underground waterways. The longest cave in the country, Pollnagollum, is at Slieve Elva, the highest of the Burren hills.

DERRYCLARE LOUGH, CONNEMARA

If you are blessed with Irish luck you will see Connemara when the sky is grey and there are more colours than you can count in the landscape, or better still, when there is a soft mist and the countryside takes on the texture that the painters of this part of Ireland love to capture. Your chances of these conditions are good, for indeed the West is not the driest of places, and the angler will be doubly grateful for a ready downpour. The rivers rise quickly after heavy rain and almost disappear in a dry season.

Thackeray described this part as "one of the most beautiful districts that it is ever the fortune of the traveller to examine", and it has changed very little since his day. There is more traffic to-day, but it could multiply many times and yet cause no serious congestion.

Beside Derryclare Lough the finest Connemara marble is quarried. It is of a soft green with stripes of yellow, white and pink, and is used in jewellery as well as pavements and facings for buildings.

BALLYNAHINCH RIVER, CO. GALWAY

A fine salmon river empties Ballynahinch Lake into Bertraghboy Bay. The lake is dotted with wooded islands, on one of which stands a ruined stronghold of the O'Flahertys, built by Donal O'Flaherty the first husband of Granuaile whose freebooting exploits on land and sea have passed into legend. On the southern shore is Ballynahinch Castle, an eighteenth-century house which has been much altered. It was for long the home of the Martin family which settled in Galway in the thirteenth century, and who ruled a vast estate of 197,000 acres, virtually all the land lying between Ballynahinch and Galway city. The most celebrated member of the family was Richard Martin (1754–1834), known as "Humanity Dick" who founded the Royal Society for the Prevention of Cruelty to Animals. The house passed from the family as a consequence of the Great Famine and had several owners, including Jam Sahib of Nawanagar—Ranjit Sinjhi the cricketer—before being converted into an hotel.

NEAR COSTELLOE, CONNEMARA

The road from Galway to Costelloe follows the north shore of Galway Bay and passes through Spiddal, where there is an attractive beach and good bathing and boating. When you arrive at Costelloe you have come to the typical Connemara scenery, open, wild and beautiful. The mountains with their changing colours provide a frame for the browns, greens and blues which in an instant may have changed to violet, grey and white. The brisk Atlantic winds fan across the Aran Islands and up the gap of Cashla Bay to spin-dry the air to an unimaginable cleanness.

In this enchanting countryside, which seems more distant from the busy city of Galway than 23 miles, the fishermen still put out to sea in currachs, the tarred canvas boats which have been used for centuries. Traditionally, each family had its own knitting stitch used in their Aran wool jerseys so that fishermen could be identified in case of disaster. The undyed and unbleached wool is virtually waterproof as it contains the natural oil of the fleece.

MINAUN CLIFFS, ACHILL, CO. MAYO

Achill Island has the best of both worlds. It has that special appeal which makes islands the ultimate in holiday resorts, a fact which has been fully exploited in the Mediterranean, and also being connected by a bridge to the mainland, it has no problems of inaccessibility in winter. The largest island off the Irish coast, it is shaped like an inverted L and is 15 miles long while its greatest breadth is 12 miles.

The cliff scenery is spectacular; the highest sea cliffs in Great Britain or Ireland are at Croaghaun, where they rise 1,950 feet from the sea. The climb to the top of Croaghaun mountain is rewarding, as at the summit, where care should be exercised, it suddenly ceases to be and falls away to the sea in a vast precipice. The Minaun Cliffs are 800 feet high but are tremendously impressive. To climb Minaun mountain is less rewarding as the summit is some distance from the edge and the cliffs are best seen from the two-mile-long strand of Tramore, which stretches towards them from the village of Keel.

KNOCKNAREA, CO. SLIGO

To the south-west of Sligo town is the isolated and enormous cone of limestone which is Knocknarea, 1,078 feet high, well worth climbing for the splendid views of the county and north to Donegal and west to Croagh Patrick in Mayo. It is crowned with a vast grey cairn of loose stones about 200 feet in diameter and 35 feet high, *Miosgan Maebha* or Maeve's Hump. The legendary Queen Maeve flourished in Connaught in the first century of the Christian era and it was she who incited the rest of Ireland to attack Ulster so that she might capture the Brown Bull of Cooley. There are several other cairns nearby, some of which have been excavated, but since it has been estimated that the stones in Maeve's mound weigh 40,000 tons, the task of examination is formidable. Yeats loved this countryside and made many landmarks of Sligo familiar throughout the English-speaking world:

The wind has bundled up the clouds high over Knocknarea
And thrown the thunder on the stones for all that Maeve can say.

On the south-west of the hill is the Glen of Knocknarea, a deep wooded chasm in the limestone with cliffs on either side of 40 to 50 feet. It is about three-quarters of a mile long and is overgrown with ivy, ferns and lush vegetation.

The Publishers wish to thank the following for permission to reproduce photographs appearing in this book:

A. & C. Photography, for pages 19, 29, 33, 37, 41, 43; Bord Faílte—Irish Tourist Board, for pages 17, 23, 47, 51, 55, 61, 63, 65, 69, 71, 73, 75, 77, 87, 91, 95, 101, 107, 109, 111; J. Allan Cash, for pages 27, 93, 103, 105; Green Studios, for page 57; Northern Ireland Tourist Board, for pages 35, 45; Kenneth Scowen, for pages 21, 25, 31, 39, 49, 53, 59, 67, 79, 81, 83, 85, 89, 97, 99.

The Author and Publishers wish to thank John Murray (Publisher) Ltd. for permission to quote from "Ireland with Emily" by Sir John Betjeman which appeared in *New Bats in Old Belfries*, 1945